D1536833

THE AVANT-GARDE DOESN'T DIE
AND NEVER SURRENDERS

NINA CASSIAN

THE AVANT-GARDE DOESN'T DIE AND NEVER SURRENDERS

— POEMS AND DRAWINGS —

Poems and Drawings Copyright © 2016 by Maurice Edwards

Postface Copyright © 2016 by Călin-Andrei Mihăilescu

Cover and Book Design by Alexandru Oprescu

All right reserved. Published by New Meridian, part of the non-profit organization New Meridian Arts, 2016

No part of this publication may be reproduced, or stored in a retrieval system, or transmitted in any form or by any means, electronic, mechanical, photocopying, recording, or otherwise, without written perimmission of the publisher, except in the case of brief quotations in reviews. For information regarding permission, write to newmeridian1@gmail.com.

Library of Congress Cataloging-in-Publication Data

The Avant-Garde Doesn't Die and Never Surrenders

Authored by Nina Cassian

ISBN-13: 978-0997603804

ISBN-10: 0997603801

2016908140

Dedicated to HUMPTY-DUMPTY
who told ALICE that he understood every POEM

CONTENTS

ALICE IN WONDERLAND

THE LITTLE PRINCE AND WINNIE THE POOH are my friends. Alice is not. I am Alice ("I am Heathcliff.") Almost everything that happened to her happened to me, in various ways: I was under-and-over-dimensioned, I encountered pools of tears, I experienced the terror of being watched by characters residing in playing cards, I was amazed by objects and chatting animals (O, so logically, so weirdly); I accepted traversing a very long dream animated by the simultaneous presence of roaring laughter and thrilling fear; I contemplated the world upside down and I voluptuously enjoyed pulling long noses at stupid solemnity.

So much myself, Alice cannot be my friend, with her ambitions, moods, arrogance and malice, behaving generally like a not very nice girl.

Fortunately, I also have something in common with her author. I am not a mathematician, yet I was always fascinated by the abstract game of numbers and by those exact phantoms called theorems. I myself wrote books for children, rather for myself than for them, I wrote them for the "immortal child" inside the all "complete" adult.

But what really brings me closest to Lewis Carroll is the incredible adventure of language—an area in which children, poets, composers, mathematicians and philosophers spread their most fantastic speculations.

Almost fifty years ago (before I ever suspected I would write for children as well), I invented "the Spargan language" and called those versified productions "spargs." The great Romanian poet, Ion Barbu, noted on the manuscript I presented him: "Nina Cassian, if you put these pranks in your book, I'll kill you! I have the right to do so, due to your incomparable talent."

He convinced me then, and I published them much later, in 1971, in a book called "Lotopoems."

Actually, those "pranks" of mine emerged decades before in another mind, on another meridian (even if just one), while my "spargs" became numerous and, somehow, "justified" by a theory concerning the existence (or pre-existence) of sonorities, beyond (or preceding) concepts.

I have to underline that "Jabberwocky" has very little in common with Christian Morgenstern's "Das grosse Lalua"—because what Lewis Carroll does is not to invent a language (there were several attempts in literature to do so and there will probably be more), but to place his inventions inside the English language (as I placed mine in the frame of Romanian).

It's like a "state within a state," integratedly to an ordinary structure, with words which—though not found in a dictionary—can be recognized as belonging to a specific mother tongue. Those "sonorities" seem to express sadness or anger or ugliness or nostalgia, they are loaded with a psychical or mental energy, with, perhaps, a multimillennial "affective etymology."

Therefore, the most appropriate homage for the anniversary of this singular work, the long dream of Alice, I thought, would be the translation into the Romanian "Spargan" of the English "Sparg"; "The Jabberwocky"—with partial annotations in the spirit of the great mathematician Martin Gardner and partially in the orbit of Humpty-Dumpty's interpretations, to which I will add the following

Glossary:

"The frumious Bandersnatch"—obviously, the character is furious and humid
Vorpal — a voracious opal
Uffish — fish's in an office state of mind
Manxome — an X-rated handsome man
Whiffling — whirlgigging waffles
Gallumphing — Hephalump galloping
    Etc. etc. etc

Nina Cassian
(*Lecture at Princeton University, early 90's*)

TO THE POET, STEPHANE ROLL — TO MY FRIEND, GHEORGHE DINU

For, look, today is the New Year,
receive this gift from me, my dear,

I place in it some windows that display
a somewhat weird but harmless array:
an egg, a polyvinyl thermofore,
an absent-minded fly,
a neighbor, one meter fabric of the Black Sea shirt,
some things with an allegro rhythmic spurt,
a moor hen, a raincoat, and, true, a jar
filled with yum marmalade from yesteryear,
a magic banderola, a midget poodle
wrapped in a layer of delicious strudel,
a star of cyclamen, a fine bone needle
fished from the throat of that white albatross,
four violins of honey, a plump fare
sliced from the moon's too evident derriere,
a little flaw, a thousand rhymes, well, toss
in a siphon, an Alpine walking stick, and oh!
androgynous, a trout from th'Orinoco,
a few sharp-edged adzes, twenty bottles
labeled, writ large, the "Era of Pericles,"
a kind of straw basket, a pungent musk species
zoologists do not recognize at all,
a fan of flames, a cascade quite tall
which stubbornly refuses to fall,
o vena cava, a wounded trochée, and a light
pitcher, filled to the brim with anthracite,
and, last but not least, a girl of halvitsa
for you to taste, my dear, oh darling Ghitsa.

EXERCISES IN STYLE

(a) Constant with Alternates

His name was, nominally, Constant,
and he had deliriums—in no small count:
He'd bought himself a car, a "Trabant,"
and trained it up and down a mount.
He wore a poncho, très elegant
(from retro time quite distant).
When he found a spot vacant
he moved into it, tremulant.
That way he grew more important.
A Casanova, dandy, dominant,
his behavior was very gallant,
with spicy women along the way.
Sometimes he even read Kant.
Other times, dared also Dante.

Those days, he looked very savant,
with his pretense—bluntly pedant.
"He's complex, but acidulant,"
stupid people did comment.
Others more extravagant
called him straightway intrigant:
"Why, his infamous intent
was to be preeminent.
Then to become distant,
and eat only bonbon fondants."
But his doctor, now current,
wrote on a loose document
he throbbed from a heart too vibrant
and scars far too penetrant.

Whereupon the younger Constant
with better plots to implement
grew much more constant.—
I put to rest my argument.

(b) Spargan Witty Couplets

Floosta shirka, floosta sharka,
joom has been crust' in the zarka!

*

The hogtsel that is hogtselled,
has no plouth and has no kell.
The hogtsella hogtsellata
has no kerba in her zata.

*

Hey, shee-shee, and then shee-shee,
don't gripee and don't furtee,
for of so much gripeerat
you'll end up unkusmiphlat.

*

You, philleek of motzoleek,
crunck yourself a bitfilleek!

(c) Forget about Cain and Abel – *Let's Write a Fable*

A somewhat petty little puppy,
with a tail like a spaghetti,
started to bark impetuously
(though he wasn't a fierce bulldog,
just a poor, meek watchdog).
And what did he do, this non-macabre?
He kept barking at a candelabra.

This candelabra (called His Highness)
asked "Who are you?"—in distress.
Doggie barked back, "Woof, woof!
Stay on the roof!
Though not ranked high in the army,
I'm not even fed salami.
Instead, I've been lionized
for being so dignified.
I bark when asked to: Bow, wow!
—of course, only when allowed—
and I know just who and what I am.
While you, you're a ridiculous item,
old as grandpa, related to Nothing.
When I raise my muzzle like a hound,
there's no danger here of a re-bound."

When the puppy finished talking,
the candelabra, now very jealous,
started to rattle his plate glass arms,
shaking fringe after fringe, what alarms!
and vituperatively, painfully pried
himself loose from the ceiling, yuppy!
Once out, and sloppy, he fell on the head
of the plebeian, uncultivated puppy.

Moral:
If you don't control your palabras,
you'll be the prey of candelabras.

(d) Western

In a dusty little town out West
there was much sun, and not much rest.
Yet with such crime and holy terror
they didn't even see their error.
Oh my! The horrible O-Kay,
with his hoodlums, so they say,
was total dictator of the town
where courage, yes, was way, way down.

Then came to town young Mr. All Right.
"Can't complain. Things now look bright."
Boasted the Sheriff: "He's like my son.
We'll show'em how the West was won,
and with his help we'll soon eradicate
O-Kay's gang, whom we all hate."

The Sheriff had a daughter so pretty
that she rivalled Nefertiti
(what was she doing in Dodge City?).
Of course, young, handsome All-Right
fell in love with her at first sight.
Overwhelmed, about to swoon,
he tumbled right into the saloon.
where O-Kay was waiting (feeling frisky
after washing down a half-bottle whiskey).
He yelled at All-Right, "Hey, you turd—"
but had no time for another word.
'cause his pistol had fallen—clink!—
out of his hand and into his drink.
(I hope you understand how risky
'tis to find a rhyme for whiskey.)

Since the fun was over and getting worse,
the Bandits left their chief sans remorse.
And All-Right married the girl in the fall.
The town breathed relief. And that is all.

8

(e) Detective Story

Back at headquarters, Scotland Yard,
the lights are on, and blazing hot.
What could have happened? Oh, it's hard
to tell. But there are crimes. A lot.
And who's the culprit? I keep guessin':
A male assassin? A female assassin?

Could be the magician, I propose,
wearing his multi-colored hose?
Or the lady with a pink hair-net
leading her little Pekingese pet?
Or maybe the bald trumpet player
from the bar, Catch-Him-Maher?
Or possibly that nice accountant
whom all of us now count on?
Or the Diva with legs divine,
Miss Lolita Frankenstein?

The cops, I think,
can't find out anything.
But Private Agent, Rex,
a handsome man in all respects,
a detective by birth, oh dearie,
whose favorite drink is a Daiquiri—
he follows all the suspects
and quickly unmasks their tricks!
There seem to be at least six.

The narrator's mistaken, I see!
Six! I'm sorry to disagree.
He's forgotten the Pekingese which
strangled a most friendly bitch...

For two months the Thames, quite cold,
flows calmly on, so I've been told,
until a new group is formed: I'm guessin'—
Male Assassins, Female Assassins?

(f) Spargan Rondel

Doin' the byng, the zbearded pikk
Had crufsted you with grassoline.
Of so much champy harbaline
He dafted all in droob and mikk.

He would've crambed, but without bleen.
Albeit unstruffed and quasi sliq,
Doin' the byng, the zbearded pikk
Had crufsted you with grassoline.

By th'end, the blind made of paleen
Amongst the willd and forochiq
Had burbured in amphetaline
And was hurdabling like a knickk

Doin' the byng, the zbearded pikk.

(g) Improper Expressions

Stud, the glyptic coxcomb,
woke up wringing wet, alone.
Much too often in his short vita
he drowned himself away,
now with Lina, now with Gita
till he turned drunken gray.
He, for sure, was really overdue
with all this hullabaloo.
In vain, he protests, you don't get drunk
that often, as if he, full of bunk,
were one of those straying about
the meadow in boots all worn out.

Not enough to be thrown into jail for,
but putting on airs, self-loving and more.
Just as he behaved his whole life long,
too big for his britches, haiku-haiphong.

In vain, Stud! Enough, girls!
Today you're all alone, soaked in whirls.

SPELLING A SPELL

Write, write, write. . .
Write
kind
kite. . .
Sing
wringing
ring. . .
Shake
sneaking
snake.
Write, write, write. . .

Gold
in his collar,
a skilled
scholar
sets
his chest
to rest
on the palimpsest. . .
Write, write, write. . .

Greedy to inhale,
a wailing
whale
swallows poems with
lines (too dark to quote 'em)
swallows Jonah's myth,
the ideal
idol
and the total
totem.

Solitary game.
Famine
without fame.
Alva
writes Alpha.
Leda
writes Beta.
Zelda
writes Delta.
Mama
writes Gamma.
Papa
writes Kappa.
As I
write Pi.

Paper white. . .
Tombstone white. . .
Write, write, write. . .

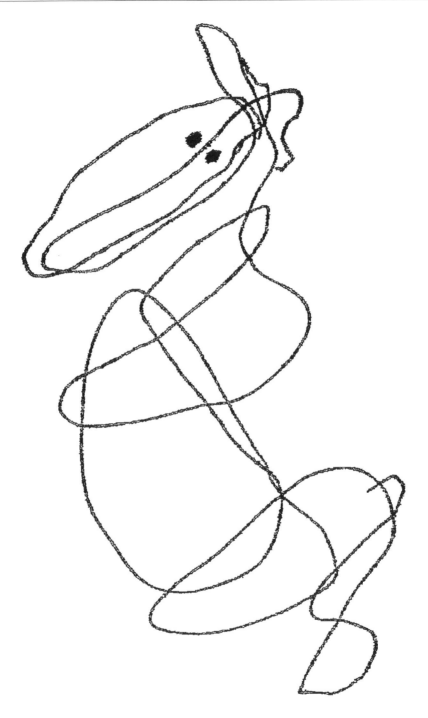

**FROM ANOTHER ERA, NOT THE FUTURE,
I'M QUITE A PROSPEROUS CREATURE**

IMAGINARY PERSONNAGES

(a) Bannibal Bura

Do you know Bannibal Bura?
He's one who prefers tempura.

When books are read on Terra Firma,
it stirs up Bannibal Bera.

Although it wasn't the Torah,
he worshipped it, Bannibal Bora.

Once in love with Scarlet O'Hara,
was volatile Bannibal Bara.

Whenever people endear a
child, it pleases Bannibal Bira.

When everything turns obscura,
it saddens poor Bannibal Bura.

(b) Chevalier Ping

He is bold, the nice Cavalier, as I've been told—
not just today or yesterday, but for a whole month—always bold.

Hey, Ping, said the Madigascaran,
and pulled out of his head a cat-scan.

On your head, I see that you can write
a report or even a symphony, is that right?

So then she, in order to prevail,
on his bald spot, plugged in a nail.

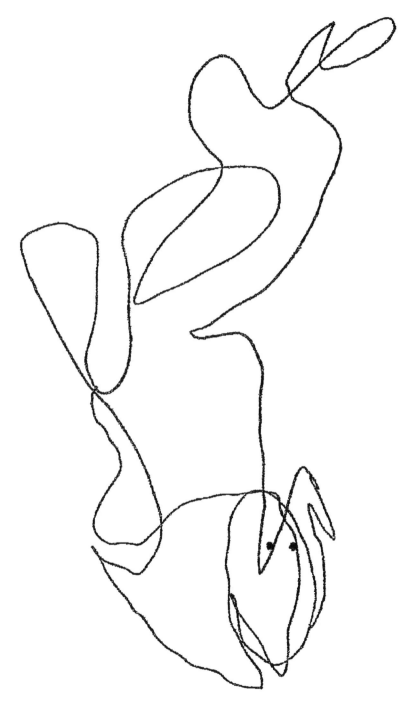

STRANGE? POINTED EARS? DISFIGURED? HOW?
LOOKS LIKE THAT TINY PUPPY "CHOW" — BOW-WOW!

(c) Differently Colored Nobles

The Duke of Alba enters Flanders
(beautiful, caressing, tender).
The same thing happens in The Netherlands,
where suave windmills turn backwards.

The Count of Dark Purple enters Innsbruck
(juvenile, timid, awestruck).
 Same thing happens to sap corrupted by a quarter,
 the uncertain aspect of blood in water.

The Prince of Vermillion enters Walloon,
and later, weeping, penetrates the lagoon.

"Get out, you Dukes & Counts! Prince, make me bereft!"
—and in their soft slippers, they gradually left.

(d) Advertisement

Don't smile,
Hyacinth!
—Glutton
is coming,
first-cousin
of Slurp,
afraid to say "Bonsoir,"
and makes you
nauseous.
—Still smiling,
Hyacinth?

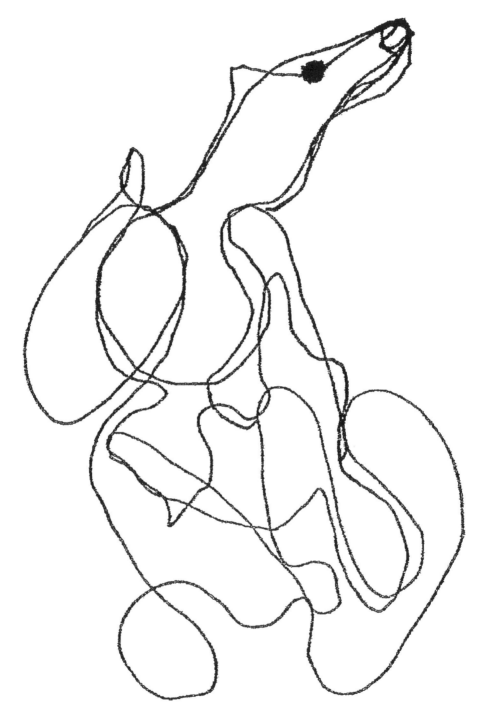

ANOTHER KNITTED DOG, I'M TOLD
THIS LITTLE DOG IS VERY BOLD.

SPARGAN BALLAD

N'other gorse is dring its candool,
untrophit, unhallowit.
Down, under the speas, the frandool
gurph that he had anthrobit.

He plevinsed with speenah tsarga
from doginste and asha.
Varicausing Kilgon Harga,
qyuldilik did only, "Gra!"

Felligated is the queenda.
Felligated very much.
Wooldy, wooldy, goarse of linda,
where is your corinder platch?

BARBARIC VARIATIONS

Beard, up there on stage, bawdy,
in a real actors' arena, and all
that shallow crowd babble:
"Bearded Lady, Bearded Lady…"

We find you with good, brave individuals,
O black-beard hermit monk, but feared
amongst all those wretched peoples—
Bluebeard, O Bluebeard.

Very brave also was the
world-renowned Barbarossa.

But the smallest barb of them all
was the Dwarf called Bashful.

ROMANCE WITH A MOSQUITO

Do you remember Fall?
It was late. I was a lady. Tall.

I had long dresses. Pink, lilac.
Gave me quite a sexy look.

Shaped like a puppy with so little,
coal eyes, and plush nose brittle.

Running from dead souls, amok,
so often, we fell out of the book.

I'm abandoning my privileges
hoping to articulate an "exegesis,"

I'm in nobody's way—no dues,
no buildings, poems or statues.

Do you remember Summer?
It was dusk. I felt grimier.

Streaming on my two sides, uselessly,
during my years of maturity.

An anopheles mosquito, flying south,
around my rebellious breast, slides
about in my puckered berry mouth.

It was dawn. And it was winter.

HYPOSTASIS: STATE OF BEING

For some time now, I've trained so hard
to pose as a Dilly-dally bird.

At first, I placed a little cylinder
next to a piece of calendar,
and perfumed myself with savor,
instead of smoking leaves of amber.

But in the end, eventually, I turned
into a Dilly-dally bird.

Since then, I wandered into Dilly-dally land,
and now they call me Mme. Cherchez de Rand.

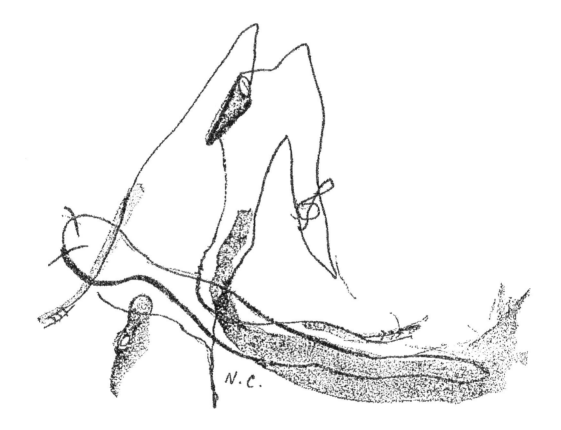

MUNCH, CRUNCH!

Dear devourer of raw meat,
I write this painted card at noon
from a place you'll hear about soon—
a wonderful planet in orbit.
        Munch, crunch ! Munch, crunch!

I'm from Planet Squared X,
whose most distinctive mark
was that you were obliged to bark
when you felt the need for food—
which is humiliating and not good.
So, nobody likes to bark.
They chew any void of any size,
 which they used to idolize.
        Munch, crunch! Munch, crunch! Munch, crunch!

But you, who know the taste of meat,
(cows, chickens, humans, too, as food,
or other beings, higher being good),
you're aware, I'm sure, of my deceit.
        Munch, crunch!

On this land, where we all crave
with our nostalgia like a wave,
I envy your retreat!
And thus my fury is complete,
Dear Devourer of Raw Meat.
        Munch, crunch!

TURBAN, THE TOM CAT

Turban the Tom Cat
is red and is gray,
and covers the head
of Pasha Ali Bey.

The Pasha did not move
his head for a year
to make Tom Cat purr
without break or fear.

From excessive strain,
stiff is Ali Bey.
Tom Cat's all smiles
either red or gray.

YES, I MAY BE CROSS-EYED.
FOR, I'VE A HAT I CANNOT HIDE.

SONNET: (IN SPARGAN LANGUAGE)

How have inmired the droadilly milande
in rockda catinate with indocrash.
So many commonzays of airs margash...
So many walnas scaterind, estrande...

Never the gooltool arphic, boonoorash,
has tofareed so many introlande.
'Twas when, with hails of air and alibande,
I beauthered on a packsy of gopash.

But now more toomnish seems to me the stena
with which the pheric golton did me roons
and its ned zoora, so elenteena...

Just vat and excitirk in ofterboons.
It zoornoes my, in nightoes, melidena
and clymphus broonzidies, rawtoons, grawtoons.

ATTENTION, CHILDREN!

Mr. Filmotek and Ms. Cocobun
at many parties were found,
but incapable of having fun
they ruined everything around.

She gets drunk and vomits. He's
accepting bribes, and utters profanities.
A third person with a certain fame
might be tempted to do just the same.

Ms. Cocobun soils everything
each time she tries to talk or sing.
Mr. Filmotek gets dressed either
as a chicken hawk or in a sweater.

I'm scared to death, oh dear,
because they ruin our fun
every time they do appear—
the Filmotek and the Cocobun.

OTHER GEOGRAPHIC REFERENCES

Somewhere on Guadalquivir,
one prefers the wine to beer.

In a town in Oklahoma,
one prefers the Met to MOMA.

In the capital Helsinki,
they have thumbs but not one pinkie.

In distant Ulan Bator,
they drink water, nothing more.

In the wild country Uganda,
they expect a baby panda.

While, of course, in Bucharest,
birds and dogs are put to rest.

THE POLYGLOT

Dear Sir, please sing me a song.
A ventriloquist lay from Hong Kong?

—Queak, queak—Thank you.
How about an Arab impromptu?

—Hark, hark—How very nice!
Now for an Eskimo song on ice.

—Brrr…—Thanks! You're so well taught.
Know something polyglot?

—Farka, larka, cutesy, tootsie.
—I salute you—admiringly.

THIS WORLD IS SO COMPLEX
IT MAKES YOU FEEL PERPLEXED.

SPARGAN PRAYER

Little tschusty, tschusty natsa,
wildó since smilingtikka, smilingtatsa,
the hap'd-hup Ashgroomter,
be his gally trehels mingfoomter,
on smilingtatsa self-genteeled,
arva mid he towerteed,
a new susa he helmeed,
with a flandel he torpeed.

A great zerka have agleed
some two hundred bellipheers,
and one hundred belliphors
of the bestest belliphars,
only grandsons of the grars.
And in birdied done by jolties
we smaled all up to the folties
and we foltied up on up
until the philly-up
till the laïs got truid
and the corvoiretors got lid.

And even the hap'd-hup Ashgroomter,
be his gally trehels mingfoomter,
did glassey on a dal
on a dal Fiandal,
and we'in unison,
the real kanson,
with ferinda, dorinda,
with pheryoana, goryana,
say gladly „Long live
Bion and Bioana!"

INTENTIONAL HALLUCINATION

Tell me when, tell me when—I do sing—
we should pull the Eyes out of our shoes,
into which they fell while outside parading,
like wet stones, like potatoes on the loose?

The Eyes of the bad young dead, at best,
circulate under asphalt-like ganglions.
I found two of them at a Friday reunion,
and hid them in the pocket of my vest.

The Eyes, if we don't find them soon ahead,
will slide mangled to the bottom of the earth.
And turn en route into a fountain of wrath
in the wind, under the fork of a crossroad.

Every day we stepped on pupils of their eyes,
like on tender glass, on gelatin waters, and
never so many marbles rolled on grassland,
never a parade so magnificent in size!

Under my heel, I crushed eyes like caviar,
which smelled to the end of the parade, so grim.
Day starts, sidewalks go up to the window rim.
Tell me when… tell me when—I implore.

EGO

It was a good year.
A few died,
but I'm alive.
A continent collapsed,
but on my street
wander dogs with pretzel tails.
Looks like a plague ahead.
Perhaps for others—
perhaps for me, a mother.

TIME OF THE COLORS

"It's time for resuscitation," the colors tell me
while deserting the lines and stripes of the fables.
"We were killed by the elegant people's look,
by pictures from the children's book."

So far so good. But the Blue, pinched
by a non-vegetarian fit of temper,
spat out and turned greenish in sickness,
the Yellow was already sick, as I remember.

While the White, losing its candid reflex,
was defending, accusing, making me a witness.
The Purple proved restless and complex,
and shivered next to the devilish Green.

And the Red, Black and other nuances more subtle,
which, when touched, made a sound quite faint,
grew eyebrows, and were caught in a babble,
as each of them voiced quite a complaint.

*

Before long, the time of the colors
could have been postponed, as you see,
but a lucky hand, maybe mine,
has, through this poem, set them free.

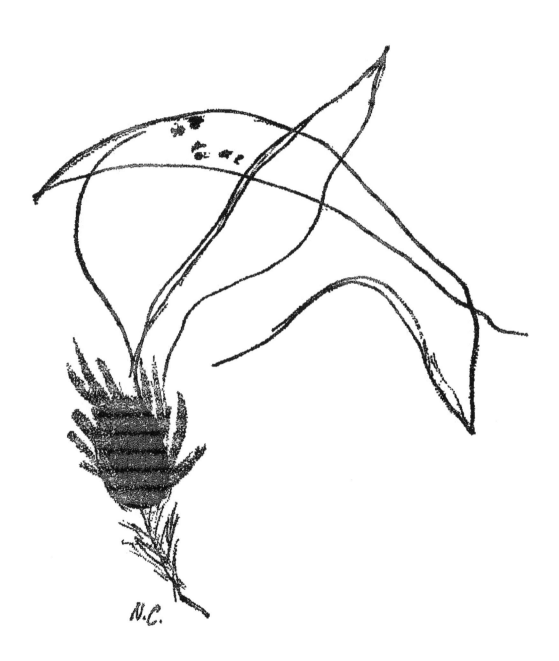

THE PLAY HOUR

It comes when it comes, the play hour.
The hand is a ribbon; the eyes a cat's dower.
The Saint and the Martyrs shrink, they said,
and get baked in their own sweetbread.

It snows. By night, we cover up in aluminum wrap,
our mineral being quaking like a cherub chap.

By day, we paint ourselves
orange or ginger,
and guide the Argonaut ship
with our forefinger.

Then time inflates
as much as life or death,
and after all that pain,
starts over again in a breath.

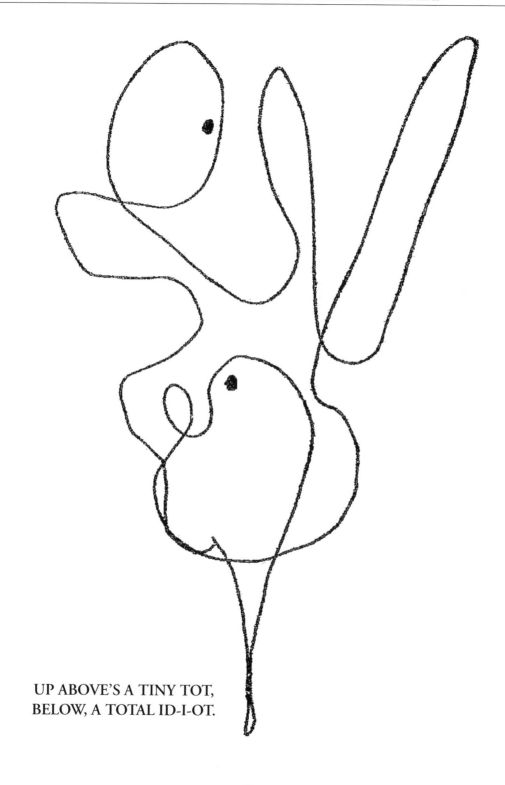

UP ABOVE'S A TINY TOT,
BELOW, A TOTAL ID-I-OT.

THREE SCHOOL COMPOSITIONS DESERVING "A's"

I:
Full moon again. The sky is clear.
Thousands of lights move down the path.
It's them. The fireflies. The peak of summer.
Bodies glow in phosphorescent mirth.

The moon is round. The sky is brighter.
Agile processions sally down roadways.
Do little insects in midst of summer
set the decorated woods ablaze?

The moon's a drum. The sky—a high void.
Behind the bushes, porcelain tones project.
Summer proffers preferable voices
through all the tiny, mute, adorable insects.

Lunar designs. Limpid vectors.
HABAKKUK! Ghosts emerge from the open tomb.

It's them. The fireflies. The peak of summer.
Bodies glow in phosphorescent bloom.

      II:
      Children, it's a winter day.
      Put on hats or maybe hoods
      so they can't be swept away
      by the harsh wind from the woods.

      Let's put on our chests the medals,
      made from snowflakes fluffy,
      and make winter lose the battle
      while we're playing lovey-dovey.

Oh, but then we howl. Tomorrow,
no "good-byes" and no "I'll see ya."
After hugs, come tears and sorrow.
(that's the general idea!)

III:
The autumn wind blows over the mountain's peak.
(Oh, dearly beloved, let me kiss your cheek.)
The autumn wind blows over waters and the plains.
(Your phosphorous mouth sparkles when it rains.)

The autumn wind blows over mountains high.
(It crawls like a lizard, our mischievous eye.)
The autumn wind blows over the big sea.
(Never was wind so real, as you can see!)

The autumn wind blows over, and down the hill.
(Come plant your kiss on me, if you will.)

The autumn wind blows over hot volcanic rods.
(I spout passages from the Upanishads.)

The autumn wind blows o'er the Chinese wall.
(I hold you close to me so you won't fall.)

The autumn wind blows sometimes wild, or mild.

(You should learn all this by heart, my child.)

LETTER

Dear Teacher   comma
Considering the great   comma
profound devotion which I have for you   comma
I beg you   comma
in view of all the possibilities   comma
to help me pass
from the class
of rigid vertebrates   comma
to the much more adaptable   comma
class of   comma
non-vertebrates of color   comma
preferably   comma
pink.

With highest regards   comma

Your devoted pupil,

Momma   comma

YOU MAY BE BEAUTIFUL AND UNIQUE,
BUT THAT'S NOT BEAUTIFUL, WHAT'S IN YOUR BEAK.

EPIDEMIC

Mr. Throat and Mrs. Jaw
sit on the porch, looking sad.
Nobody comes to visit them now,
as if the entire street were dead.

Mr. Throat coughed loudly by night:
"This entire village is impolite."
But Mrs. Jaw sniffed: "How wrong are you!
The entire village is thick with flu."

APOCALYPSE WITH FIGURES.

THE BOYLE FAMILY

How far back does it go, your specie!
Look, there they are again, sitting at table:
The Ulcer, the Boil and little Boyle Baby.
A furious summer begins. What a fable.

Clusters of grapes in the vineyards drying.
Degenerate cats and swallows decaying.
Yet as long as they reign hereabout
 in the fruits, the silent worms re-sprout.

I see them. I sicken slowly,
I have no choice. There's Mme. De Boyle,
her heavy spit, thick as sorbet, still
covering my window entirely.

In the doorway stands Father Boyle,
his long beard parted in two.
On his father's chest hides Baby Boyle,
there where there is no hair. Such ado.

What a lot of creatures there—
that terrible Boil family,
plus a younger boy: little Boily.

Good Earth, why do you scare me?

WITH ALL THOSE STRANGERS EVERYWHERE,
WHY ARE YOU SO UNHAPPY THERE?

FORM AND CONTENT

Into a clay recipient
I introduced a content.

But the silly content, I see,
declined to fit in entirely.

More than half of it, alack,
stuck out loosely from its back.

While th' other half hung from its head
and shouted; "I don't fit, 'ere dead!"

I took a log struck down by storm
to push the content into form.

When I prayed God to stop the stress,
the log split into splinters—oh, bless!

I called the poet, and said: "Get in!
Do your job slowly, future Djinn!"

The poet crawled into the vessel,
but the unfortunate content
stayed out, the recreant pestle.

YOU ABOVE AND ME BELOW —
LOOK AT US, WE'RE QUITE A SHOW.

SPARGAN DIRGE

Arrough, arrough,
the mord more lift, more arthough.
Th'alna still hangars in zway,
th'elt more aviled batheslay.

Arrough, arrough,
who was my ast malibro?
Who has angired props of louth,
by hornings of filligan's outh?

Strams the akoustric owproond.
Th'elt still avils in the hoond.
Arrough, arrough,
the mord is no longer arthough.

FRIENDSHIP

A Kangaroo named Callahan
encountered an orang-u-tan,
who said: "I'm sure of it, I vouch,
your baby's happy in your pouch.."

"…And you, you're never cold, I can attest,
because you wear a thick and hairy vest!"

Since then, they launched according to a plan,
the fashion KANGORANGUTAN!

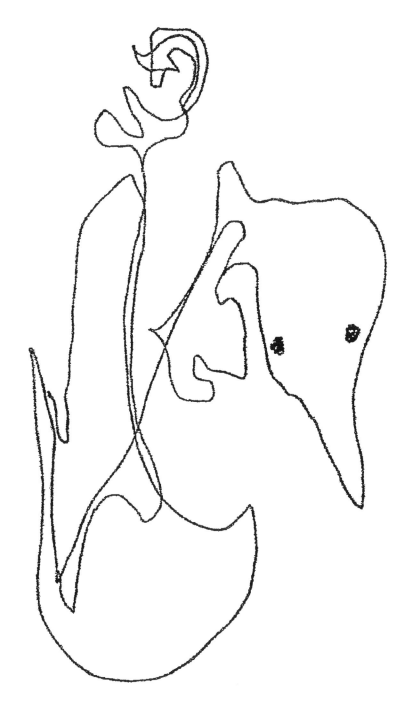

WHAT GIVES YOU THE WILL TO LIVE,
IS THAT SHE'S SO INQUISITIVE.

LIQUID

Liquids dwindle, don't you see,
and sliver down in channels, *oui!*

From there, they soar up to the sun,
Later, in high mountains, start again to run.

Up on heights, when liquids fade,
they emerge as great cascades.

and when liquids swell, I wish
the seas would then fill up with fish.

So, dwindling, growing, passing through,
liquids liquidate the land around you.

WHAT WERE YOU FISHING FOR?

In the Strait of Skagerrak
—blue fish, green fish, pink fish, black.

In the Strait of Kattegat
—catfish (four) and one fishcat.

In the dark Strait of Magellan
—one honest, one a felon.

In the white Strait of Gibraltar
—perfect trout, they never falter.

In the reddish Strait of Bering
—a smoked salmon and a herring.

In the Gulf of Mexico
—breaded crabs, ready to go.

In the friendly China Sea
—tiny oysters, hard to see.

In the nice Bay of Biscay
—just one shrimp. But that's O.K.

That was last year. Now I wish
no more waters, no more fish.

WHAT HAVE WE HERE? SOMETHING THAT CRAWLS?
OF COURSE, MY DEAR — SOME LITTLE ANIMALS.

ANOTHER EXERCISE IN STYLE

His name was actually Gary,
he never intended to marry—
not to Mary, quite contrary!

Then he changed his name to Fred,
and remained a bachelor instead.
Next he called himself Alfonso,
wearing just a simple poncho.

Then again his name was Grant—
he became an intrigant.
Finally he changed to Hughes,
and tried out other hues.

Gary changed his name too many times.
Spare me! I won't look for other rhymes.

TO AN INGRATE (IN SPARGAN)

I'm brobding you, doorvangèd and polishtaled noranga,
I'm brobding you to faltzel your vortface and to swooy
the multimlabbial moshka on a crepitted hanga
and to jomeeze your trigga by one hussardic huy.

I'm brobding you, with th'azkah vagleena and altera,
to 'ntroughther the eldegance of a letusk atsod
whom ardous tentezina of the humblideous serra
and pentiferges th'hystra in which whoordogies Dod.

ECHOES OF DADA

(after Tristan Tzara)

—She hanged herself
Nina, the blond Nina,
at night, from the pole.

—Because of so many a "no"
her name passed
into a double "Da".   ("Yes")
pronounced "Dada".   ("Yes Yes")

Nina Knew

FINALLY THE BATTLE OF WATERLOO was coming to a close. General Cambronne, commander of the last of Napoleon's Old Guard, was about to be made prisoner by the Brits. *Merde!*, he said, unarmed sources reported. French is a language poor in swearwords, so *merde* carries, Atlas-like, a load of meanings; in this case, either 'go screw yourselves! (to the Brits who'd asked him to surrender); or 'shit!' (Hollywood antagonists' last word of choice); or 'to hell with you/it!', etc. Countless times did Cambronne deny having said either *Merde!* Or the more famous and patriotic, *La Garde meurt et ne se rend pas!* (The Guard dies and doesn't surrender!). Another French General, Pierre-Etienne Michel claimed having uttered that greatest exit line in modern warfare. But that was yet another rhetorical blunder volunteering to spice up history's irony. Unlike the alluded to medieval hero, Roland, who died with the *arrière-garde* of Charlemagne's army trying to hold the myriad of Moors at Roncesvalles, bad luck had Michel (and Cambronne) survive Waterloo. The air thickens at the end of wars and words fly by astonished. The last bullet dreams of dealing the mortal blow to the enemy; the last word, to be carved in titanium. The zone that buffers the turfs of battle from those of rhetoric is itself a mine field filled with laughing gas. That high-order imposition, "To die and not surrender" makes survival unheroic and brands life *misérable*. One doesn't die when one should; one dies when one can, said Borges.

The Avant-Garde Doesn't Die and Never Surrenders tells the opposite story. It says that one frees oneself when one can and should.

When Nina Cassian, *grande dame* of Romanian letters came to the States, the year was 1985 and the iron maiden wrought behind the Curtain had left too little space to maneuver. The absurd meant then-and-there the exhaustion one met with on one's way to sense, and Romania was feeding on the abundant absurd it produced. How to get out of that messy centripetal spin—that mass of un-happenings and prophecies of doom that meant Nothing? Via the adventurous spirit of nonsense—Lewis Carroll's Jabberwocky march, Tristan Tzara's DadaEast push, or the strata of Surrealism piling up one atop the Other. Yet nonsense can't go on forever, unless it gives up and wishes to be crowned as its opposite. Another nonsense only can arrest it: religion, for instance, or literary glory, exile or suicide. Nina toyed with the idea of suicide, nursed glory's vanity, shunned religion and chose exile. She knew how to board the avant-garde getaway vehicle, deflower the iron maiden and run west. She found the west both attractive and repellent—some sacred cows gift poisoned milk. How would the west feed the poet, that charming being vehemently glued to a world uncharmed by arms and speed, phlegmatic and spilled blood, hard machines and (lack of) money? In West we trust when only in the East, but what would the avant-garde getaway vehicle keep running on in the flat-futured West?

Nina knew the avant-garde's joyful flights and chivalrous desperation. And she despised escapism, the lowbrow running away from the avant-garde's push through and toward new lands of imagination. She was not the first at that. She was coming from a culture that had flooded the West with mis-baptized Jewish-Romanian avant-gardists who were to die at Auschwitz, like Benjamin Fondane (or Barbu Fundoianu, born Benjamin Wechsler, 1898-1944), or in Paris, like Tristan Tzara (born Samuel Rosenstock, 1896-1963), Ilarie Voronca (born Eduard Marcus, 1903-1946), Victor (born Viktor) Brauner (1903-1966), Eugène Ionesco (born Eugen Ionescu,1909-1994), Gherasim Luca (born Salman Locker, 1913-1994), Paul Celan (born Paul Antschel, 1920-1970), and Isidore Isou (born Ioan-Isidor Goldstein, 1925-2007). Out of desperation, three great poets jumped off the *salon des réfugiés* into the Seine, and thus met their deaths, *sous le pont Mirabeau*, each two zodiacs apart: Ilarie Voronca in 1946, Paul Celan in 1970 and the StranJew Gherasim Luca in 1994.[1] Paris became deserted. Nina went to New York, instead. There she lived on Roosevelt Island, in the musty middle of th'East River. That river is too profligately wide to fathom its ancestor meandering slowly through Paris in search of poetic fodder. Nina knew she would be safe here—she'd come too late to drown.

Nina knew: the avant-garde must never tire of tickling the dead souls chuckling along the Ministry of Serious Affairs' halls. That's a tall order—if culture is play, the avant-garde must be its essence. The avant-garde, which grants only a dismally small distance between practice and theory, in practice neither derives from theory nor follows nor precedes it. She was not a typical avant-gardist, one who'd put on revolutionary fatigues to ruffle the past. Sick with the "historical" avant-gardes' hammering out manifesto after manifesto, she was forewarned by the likes of Marinetti (turned Mussolingian) and of Tzara, Breton and some others (turned Stalinist), that the historical avant-gardes soon got engaged in those most disciplinarian lines and ides of March. Those avant-gardes pushed hard glory's gates to become "historical" and thus quickened utopia's fates, which

---

[1] Gherasim Luca used to call himself *un étranjuif*, a StranJew. For those who like their words unpacked, an *étrange Juif* is a strange Jew.

had switched from the counter-fanatic lightheartedness of Thomas More and Rabelais to the fatal seriousness of Marx and Ford.

Nina went against the grain. After joining the privileged bunch of socialist-realists throughout the dark fifties, writing smoothly along the Communist Party lines, yet showing grace while in power and uncommon helpfulness toward her misplaced fellow writers, she progressively disentangled herself from this rough past. Coming out clean was strenuous; after more than fifty years and fifty volumes of poetry—for children, for playful grown-ups, for the melancholy and, print-permitting, for those taking sabbaticals with the avant-garde's imp—some stayed nonplussed, some others unforgiving, and many were taken by her poetry. And so stayed Nina (born Renée Annie Cassian-Mătăsaru [Galați, 1924 – New York City, 2014]): a complex and contradictory, first-class character in the history of Romanian literature, a woman of many lives whose avant-garde was not a way away from the past of others, but her own.

Nina was the girl who composed her first song at five and somehow never grew up, although she kept composing and drawing until dusk; all of her was as educated as her voice; she was the blossoming woman who kept budding through loves and other fires; she was the muse and the poet; she was reluctant to let go of any of these; rather than having one followed by the other and thus allow them to define her artsy trajectory, she projected each of them into the infinite; Infinina is a magic encyclopedia of being.

While Nina was not a hard core avant-gardist, she became an essential one. That's to say that, for her, the categorical imperative was expressed as responsibility to gratuitousness. In search of freedom, mystics jump out of this world; post-moderns out of the actual into the eventual e-malaise of the digital; but avant-gardists rush to the readers to take them by the hand in dizzying dances and playful flights and keep them at bay from time's rot. The avant-gardists jump into the beyond inside—or, for those prone to technicalities, the transcendent at the heart of the immanent.

Framed from within by Nina's delightfully witty drawings, *The Avant-Garde Doesn't Die and Never Surrenders* collects her most famous Romanian avant-garde poems, written over six decades (1947-2007), almost all of which she translated towards the end of her life. Nina was a language poet *avant la lettre* who was well translated into English even[2]

---

[2] *Blue Apple*, trans. Eva Feiler, New York, 1981; *Lady of Miracles*, trans. Laura Schiff, Berkeley, 1988; and *Call Yourself Alive*, trans. Brenda Walker and AndreeaDeletant, London, 1988.

before adding to her personae that of an American poet.[3] The latter was a process, as Billy Crystal would call it, not easy—"Compared to my struggle with English | Hercules was a honeychild…."—nor unworthy—"My tongue—[is] forked like a snake's | but without deadly intentions | just a bilingual hissing."[4]

The result of this bilingual hissing, which you can hear-see in this volume, is a cluster of deliberately minor texts. At the antipodes of the legislative push of Futurist and Surrealist machos, Nina's soft avant-gardism is funny, is light, it whispers in this shouting country, it allows itself some *faux pas*, some coquettish hesitations, which are also traps for the reader ready to put on a judge's robe.

Oh, reader, dear reader, suspend your dis-funniness! Let go of your habits (bad, good, and habitual) and get on with Nina's play! You will feel light and right and free, for now you can and should. Why would I get tacky and pedantic and point you in the direction of this or that text from this volume? You have it in your hands, those capable of turning the pages. You get it, sure you do:
—Bannibal Bura likes tempura and Bannibal Bara loves Scarlet O'Hara;
—the poet Stephane Roll is the same Gheorghe Dinu[5] to whom the young poet gifts herself on New Year's 1947 (or was it '48)?;
—the kangorangutan is not out of fashion's cards;
—in the nice Bay of Biscay / just one shrimp. But that's O.K.;
—She hanged herself | Nina, the blond Nina, / at night, from the pole;
—North of Sparta is Athens; Spargan is spoken further North;

You get the Spargan language crafted by Nina in the wake of Lewis Carroll's Jabberwocky (a poem whose language she translated into exhilarating Romanian). In the spirit of Morgenstern and Queneau and Foarță, her seven Spargan poems here enlarge language to the point of nonsense, of a sphincterless universal meant to return it to its garden-fresher being. '*A sparge*' means 'to break' in Romanian; *limba spargă*—Spargan, or 'Breakalese.'

---

[3] *Life Sentence*, ed. William Jay Smith, New York & London, 1990; *Cheerleader for a Funeral*, trans. Nina Cassian and Brenda Walker, London & Boston, 1992; *Take My Word for It*, New York, 1998; *Continuum*, New York, 2008; and, now, this volume.

[4] "Invitation au voyage," and "Language," respectively, both in *Take My Word for It*: 45, 69.

[5] Publicist Gheorghe Dinu (pen name of the playful poet Stephan Roll, 1903-1974), one of the early Romanian avant-gardists, edited (with Ilarie Voronca) the one and very influential issue of the journal *75HP* (1924), and contributed to the main avant-garde publications of the ebullient 1920s Bucharest: *Punct* (Point) *Integral*, and *unu* (one), before turning to the left of the political spectrum and staying there.

Call it what you want: you can't be wrong, for it disrupts the language only to let it re-construct itself through you, dear reader. Hey, not as broken English! As English reborn! Just Google-translate that, or kill it with a gun: it will laugh at you until you lay down your weapons and inter-faceless dictionaries, and start laughing, too.

One more thing; or two. Looking over Nina's translations, I first thought that she, the ultimate musician, was losing her famous sense of prosody. Some lines were coming out in LimpEnglish, some were running out of air. So I dared give them some pre-Wallace Stevens melodic fixes. Some came out right, well, right like an obituary. But as I fear all funeral fanfares, I stepped back and eventually got it. Nina's translations were avant-gardiste. She would translate her clean Romanian prosody into strata that English had let go of since Shakespeare's sonnets and since the lullabied babies have grown into taxpayers. She would go back decades to dig out her poems and re-avant-gardize (argh!) them in English. She did so to be a tad scandalous, yet classy, self-pampering, yet provoking you, dear reader, to correct her (as I foolishly did). Nina's avant-garde poetry goes through wars but, instead of imposing a peaceful resolution, it shows that a dialectical excuse is only as rhetorical as the choice between death and surrender—a load of Cambronne.

Some do as tails committed to their comets, some tell the bullets not to rush, some run away from the pile of rubble growing skyward, but in the end Nina would have none of these. If history were fair, she would have been born in the late Seventeenth Century, when Versailles was still young, to both enjoy and craft the age of hedonism, to brush impenitently with the *mots d'esprit*, in dark green taffeta and silk shoes, as a mistress of the chiaroscuro having each syllable wink at the reader. As she was not to be carried in the gilded carriage of Pascal's French, she had to do it all by herself, me-andering between the irrespirable protipendada and the Communist wooden tongue. Free within that impossible space, she warns you, reader: "Doin' the byng, the zbearded pikk | Had crufsted you with grassoline. | Of so much champyharbaline | [S]he dafted all in droob and mikk."

Călin-Andrei Mihăilescu

32489060R00043

Made in the USA
Middletown, DE
06 June 2016